Little Grey Rabbit
Makes Lace

Alison Uttley
pictures by Margaret Tempest

Collins

William Collins Sons & Co Ltd
London · Glasgow · Sydney · Auckland
Toronto · Johannesburg

First published 1950
© text The Alison Uttley Literary Property Trust 1986
© illustrations The Estate of Margaret Tempest 1986
This arrangement © William Collins Sons & Co Ltd 1986
Cover decoration by Fiona Owen
Decorated capital by Mary Cooper
Alison Uttley's original story has been abridged for this book.
Uttley, Alison
Little Grey Rabbit makes lace. —
Rev.ed — (Little Grey Rabbit books)
I. Title   II Tempest, Margaret
III. Series
823'912 [J] PZ7

ISBN 0-00-194214-X

Made and Printed in Great Britain by
William Collins Sons and Co Ltd, Glasgow

FOREWORD

Of course you must understand that Grey Rabbit's home had no electric light or gas, and even the candles were made from pith of rushes dipped in wax from the wild bees' nests, which Squirrel found. Water there was in plenty, but it did not come from a tap. It flowed from a spring outside, which rose up from the ground and went to a brook. Grey Rabbit cooked on a fire, but it was a wood fire, there was no coal in that part of the country. Tea did not come from India, but from a little herb known very well to country people, who once dried it and used it in their cottage homes. Bread was baked from wheat ears, ground fine, and Hare and Grey Rabbit gleaned in the cornfields to get the wheat.

The doormats were plaited rushes, like country-made mats, and cushions were stuffed with wool gathered from the hedges where sheep pushed through the thorns. As for the looking-glass, Grey Rabbit found the glass, dropped from a lady's handbag, and Mole made a frame for it. Usually the animals gazed at themselves in the still pools as so many country children have done. The country ways of Grey Rabbit were the country ways known to the author.

Grey Rabbit sat at her cottage door one fine morning with her work-basket at her side and the scissors on the doorstep. She was making a nightcap for Mrs Hedgehog out of a little pink handkerchief. Hare had picked it up on the common, dropped from somebody's pocket. Grey Rabbit decided it was just right for a nightcap. She snipped the edge neatly and sewed a hem, shaping it to fit Mrs Hedgehog's head. Her little needle flew in and out of the linen and her stitches were so small they were almost invisible.

It was very quiet in the cottage, for Hare and Squirrel had gone out together across the fields to visit the Speckledy Hen, but in the trees all the birds were singing.

There was a flutter of wings and Robin the postman flew down with his letter-bag, from which he took a little green-leaf letter.

"You're lucky today, Grey Rabbit. Here's a letter."

"A letter for me?" cried Grey Rabbit, dropping her sewing.

"It's not very important. I read it first," said the Robin. "I should have come at once if it had been URGENT."

"Dear Robin," laughed Grey Rabbit. "I can't even read it, it has such crooked letters."

"It says: 'Riddle-me-ree,
            I'm coming to tea,'"
said the postman. "Never a please or thank you, or anything."

"Who sent it?" asked Grey Rabbit, turning it over and looking at the back. Then she saw the letter F scribbled on the stalk.

"Ah! It's from Fuzzypeg," she cried. "He knows he is always welcome."

"I might have guessed! I saw the little hedgehog go past with his schoolbag early this morning. I'll say good-bye, now, Grey Rabbit, and go back to my garden."

The Robin flew away with his empty postbag flapping behind him, and Grey Rabbit took up her sewing. The needle had fallen out, and she hunted in the grass for it.

"Cuckoo! Cuckoo!" cried a small squeaky voice, and there stood Fuzzypeg with his pointed nose pushed between the bars of the gate.

"Come along, little Fuzzypeg. I've just had a nice letter from you. I am so glad you've come."

"I thought I would and I did," said Fuzzypeg. "It was a holiday, and I didn't know, so I've been finding presents all day."

He slipped his paw in his left pocket and brought out a robin's pin-cushion.

"It's the reddest pin-cushion I've ever seen on a rose-bush. It's for you to stick your pins in, Grey Rabbit."

Little Grey Rabbit thanked him and put it in her workbasket, but Fuzzypeg dived deep into his right pocket and brought out a double-daisy. Then he went to his left pocket for a peacock butterfly, and to his right for a ladybird in a spotted cloak. Finally from the left pocket came a green-shining beetle.

"Oh, thank you, Fuzzypeg," said Grey Rabbit, as all these things appeared. The butterfly flew on the workbox and sunned its wings. The ladybird settled on the pink linen cap. The little emerald beetle walked straight to the needle and stood by it.

"Oh, look! He's found my lost needle," cried Grey Rabbit. "Isn't he clever!"

"I thought he was a special beetle," agreed Fuzzypeg. "That's why I brought him to see you."

He ran indoors and fetched a stool and sat down by his friend's side. He watched Grey Rabbit thread her needle and make her tiny stitches.

"What are you making, Grey Rabbit?" he asked.

"Hush! It's for your mother," she whispered. "It's a nightcap."

"She *will* be pleased, Grey Rabbit." Fuzzypeg stroked the soft linen admiringly. "She made a wish for a nightcap."

"Grey Rabbit," he continued, "I've seen something today."

"Yes? What is it?" Grey Rabbit smiled at the eager face turned towards her.

"I went across the common early this morning, to post your letter, and do you know, there was lace hanging on the gorse."

"Lace? What kind of lace?"

"Very nice lace, silver and grey, all dangling from the prickles. Where did it come from, Grey Rabbit?"

"I expect it was the spiders' weaving. They are clever creatures, Fuzzypeg. They hang out their silver webs in the bushes to catch sunbeams."

"I tried to bring you some, but it all curled up to nothing," said Fuzzypeg.

"You can't carry it, Fuzzypeg."

"I think my mother would like some lace on her cap. Can you make it, Grey Rabbit?"

"I can't make lace," sighed Grey Rabbit. "I'll ask Squirrel when she comes home. I can hear voices in the fields now. Squirrel and Hare will soon be here."

"Riddle-me-ree, I want my tea," sang Fuzzypeg, leaping up, and he and Grey Rabbit ran indoors to set the table. Fuzzypeg toasted the muffins, and Grey Rabbit washed the lettuces and radishes, and put them on the little plates. She brought a cake from the larder and a loaf of currant bread from the bread-mug. She was just making the tea when the garden gate rattled and Squirrel and Hare came racing up the path into the house. Fuzzypeg hid under the table. He suddenly felt shy.

"Is tea ready, Grey Rabbit? We are hungry!" cried Squirrel, tossing a bunch of flowers on the table.

"Grey Rabbit! Grey Rabbit!" shouted Hare. "We saw Speckledy Hen and she sent two eggs for your tea. I rolled one down a hill, and it went so fast I couldn't catch it."

"Not till it was broken," explained Squirrel.

"And where's the other egg?" asked Grey Rabbit.

"Well, we tried to see if it could swim, and it was drowned in the stream among the forget-me-nots," said Hare sadly.

Just then Hare noticed the little pink cap lying neatly folded on the workbasket. He snatched it up and set it on his long ears.

Then he danced round singing:

> "A hunting-cap for me.
> A hunting-cap for me.
> I'll catch the wicked Fox
> And put him in a box,
> And serve him up for tea."

"No, it's for me," cried Squirrel, grabbing the cap from Hare and perching it on her own red head.

"It isn't for either of you," shrieked an indignant, muffled voice, and Fuzzypeg scrambled out and pulled Squirrel's tail. "It's for my mother." He was half-crying.

"Hallo, Fuzzypeg! What are you doing here?" cried Hare.

"I've come for tea, and it's a hunting-cap for my mother, it is," sobbed Fuzzypeg.

"It's a nightcap for Mrs Hedgehog, made out of the handkerchief you found, Hare," explained Grey Rabbit. "It's to keep her warm when she looks at the new moon."

"My mother always makes a c-c-c-c-curtsey to-o th-the n-n-new m-m-moon and she gets a w-w-wish," sobbed Fuzzypeg. "She w-w-wished for a hunt-hunt-nightcap and th-this is it."

"Now come along and have tea, all of you," said Grey Rabbit. "Fuzzypeg must have the biggest muffin, and the slice of cake with cherries on top."

"Squirrel, can you make lace?" asked
Fuzzypeg, suddenly cheerful, as he gobbled up
his muffin.

"No, I can't, but I know where Queen
Anne's Lace grows," answered Squirrel.

"Queen Anne's Lace? What's that?"
Fuzzypeg stared at Squirrel.

"It's the foamy white flower that fills the
hedgebanks and ditches, where you hide
when anyone goes past," said Hare.

"Oh, yes. I know it. I've often hidden in
it."

"What do you want lace for, Fuzzypeg?" said Hare.

"It's for my mother's nightcap, to go round the edge," said Fuzzypeg.

Grey Rabbit explained about the gossamer lace which hung on the hedges and gorsebushes. They all shook their heads, saying nobody could make lace except the spiders and perhaps the fieldmice.

"I'll go tomorrow to visit the fieldmice and the spiders, Fuzzypeg, and when I have some lace I will trim the cap ready for the new moon."

"Yes, and when my mother makes her wish, I'll pop it on her head. Won't she be surprised!" laughed Fuzzypeg, clapping his hands.

When tea was over, Fuzzypeg ran home. Grey Rabbit finished sewing the cap, and Squirrel tried it on again.

"It would be lovely with lace round the edge," said she, running to look at herself in the glass.

The next day Grey Rabbit knocked at the door of the little house where the fieldmice lived. Through the open door she could see washing before the fire and a basket of sewing on the table. They were always busy because there were so many children.

"Excuse me, Mrs Mouse, can you make lace?" asked Grey Rabbit, looking at the frills and little garments hanging there.

"Lace, Miss Grey Rabbit? Oh no! We always bite the edges of our frills to make them shaggy, but we cannot weave lace."

So Grey Rabbit went to the common to ask the spiders about it. They took no notice of her. They were spinning their silken webs and running in and out of the golden gorse flowers, and they had no time for the rabbit.

"I don't think anybody can make lace," said she. So the pink nightcap lay in the workbasket, and the moon grew larger and larger till it was full moon. Then it began to wane, and Grey Rabbit was afraid the new moon would appear like a thin horn in the sky, and Mrs Hedgehog would have no lace on her cap to greet it.

One sunny day Hare was coming home from a journey, and he took a short cut through the village.

From the schoolroom came singing, and Hare listened as he passed the door.

"Queen Anne, Queen Anne,
She sat in the sun,
Making of lace till the day was done.
She made it green, she made it white,
She made it of flowers and sunshine
    and light.
She fastened it on a stalk so fine,
She left it in the hedgerow to shine.
Queen Anne's Lace. Queen Anne's Lace.
You find it growing all over the place."

At the door of a pretty cottage, all among roses and lilies, sat an old lady, and something about her made Hare stop still.

She was sitting on a low chair in the porch, with a dark pillow on her lap, and her fingers were moving as swiftly as two darting birds. Little brown wooden bobbins, like toys, with glass beads dangling down, were flying to and fro, and spidery threads were twisting as if a wind blew them.

"Good morning, Mr Hare," she called, nodding her old head in its sun-bonnet, and tapping with her toes.

"Good morning, Queen Anne," said Hare.

"Miss Susan," said the old lady. "That's my name."

"Good morning, Queen Anne," repeated Hare. "Please, what are you doing?"

"What do you think, Mr Hare?" laughed Miss Susan.

"I think you are either playing a tune or making Queen Anne's Lace, like the flowers in the hedges," said Hare.

"Clever Hare! I am making lace," said Miss Susan.

Hare stood close to her, and stared at her nimble fingers, following the pattern pricked on a strip of paper laid on her lace-pillow. Every little wooden bobbin was cut in a charming shape, with coloured beads dangling at the ends.

As she worked, the old lady talked to Hare and told him about lace-making. He told her about Grey Rabbit, and the cap she had made for Fuzzypeg's mother.

He would have been there all day if there hadn't been the tinkle of a bell in the schoolroom, and the laughter of children pouring down the road, free from lessons. They gave a shout when they saw Hare, but Hare saw them in time. He ran for his life, with his ears laid flat and his big eyes starting with fright.

"I won! I won!" cried Hare, as he dashed into the cottage. "They ran and they ran, but they couldn't catch me."

"Yes, of course, but where have you been, Hare?" asked Grey Rabbit.

"I've been watching Queen Anne make lace, and I can tell you all about it."

"Hare! Have you really discovered Queen Anne?" cried the delighted Squirrel.

"She lives in the village and she showed me how to make lace. You want a pillow."

"There's a pillow on my bed," said Grey Rabbit, scampering upstairs to fetch it.

"And you want bobbins," continued Hare. "Not cotton reels, but long bobbins, all carved with pretty beads on the ends."

"I'll make them," said Rat, from the open door. "I'll carve them for you."

"And I'll get the beads," squeaked Fuzzypeg, peering round after Rat.

"You will want a paper pattern with flowers or something pricked on it," said Hare.

"We'll make the paper pattern, Grey Rabbit, with our sharp teeth."

Hare frowned as the family of fieldmice crowded in the doorway.

"And you will want some fine long threads to make the lace," he said.

"There is plenty of sheep's wool in the hedges," Squirrel cried. "I can twist fine threads with it."

So the Rat made the lace-bobbins, some from pieces of bone and some from wood. Fuzzypeg hung beads of hawthorn and berries at the ends for weights. The fieldmice made lace patterns, pricking the paper with rows of bees and flowers. Squirrel wound the wool thread on the bobbins.

Then everybody came to see Grey Rabbit make lace.

The little rabbit sat at the door with her pillow on her knee, and the bobbins hanging down. She tossed the bobbins over and crossed the threads and moved the pins down the paper pattern, while they all watched her paws. A tiny strip of lace appeared, and it took the shape of a bee. On she went, and a flower came, and then another bee. She made a row of bees and flowers, with a wavy edge to the sheep's-wool lace like flowing water.

Grey Rabbit's paws, which had moved slowly at first, now flashed backward and forward, and the piece of lace hung down like gossamer.

Then Grey Rabbit sewed it round the nightcap for Mrs Hedgehog, just in time for the rising of the new moon.

Mrs Hedgehog went outside to see the moon. She stood in the chilly evening light, and when she saw the lovely pale sickle of the moon in the sky, she solemnly bowed three times. Fuzzypeg, standing by her side, bowed too.

"I wish for a nightcap to keep my head warm," murmured Mrs Hedgehog.

Then, from behind his back, Fuzzypeg brought out the pink linen nightcap with sheep's-wool lace. He popped it on his mother's head, and how delighted she was!

"I have never seen such a lovely cap in all my born days," cried Mrs Hedgehog, hugging Fuzzypeg. "Real lace, with bees and flowers all round the edge. It must have been made by a Fairy."

So that is how Grey Rabbit made lace.

In the village Miss Susan told a strange story.

"Do you mean to tell us that a Hare came to watch your lace-making?" asked the neighbours.

"He did indeed, and he was a very intelligent Hare. He called me Queen Anne," said Miss Susan proudly.

Nobody believed Miss Susan, but Robin the postman, who was sitting on a spade handle, heard this, and he told Hare.

"We'll hang a piece of lace on Queen Anne's door-knob. Then she can show the village," said Hare.

Grey Rabbit made the most beautiful strip of lace, and Robin the postman hung it on the door-knob of the thatched cottage.

"Now look!" cried the old lady triumphantly, showing it to her neighbours. "This isn't my work. Did you ever see such lace as this? Grey Rabbit must have made it and Hare told her how to do it and I told Hare."

"We'll put it in the village museum," they said. "It's the strangest lace ever known, and as fine as a fairy's work."

There it lies, in a glass case, with a Queen Elizabeth shilling and a stone arrow-head. People stare at its beauty, and wonder who made it, but we know, don't we?